PARATAXIS

Matt Hill

BlazeVOX [books]

Buffalo, New York

Parataxis by Matt Hill

Copyright © 2008

Published by BlazeVOX [books]

Printed in the United States of America

Book Design by Geoffrey Gatza

First Edition

ISBN: 1-934289-88-4
ISBN 13: 978-1-934289-88-4
Library of Congress Number: 2008938104

BlazeVOX [books]
14 Tremaine Ave
Kenmore, NY 14217

Editor@blazevox.org

publisher of weird little books

BlazeVOX [books]

blazevox.org

2   4   6   8   0   9   7   5   3   1

B   X

This book is dedicated to the memory of my mother, Estelle Marie Hill (1923-1981) - it was she who gave me my first dictionary and encouraged me in the use of the imagination.

Appreciative thanks to the Sanchez family, who generously allowed me to loiter on the premises while I worked on this project; to Scott Clements, James Maughn, and Andrew Joron, for the prepress review and comments; and to Geoffrey Gatza, for the gracious invite. I truly am grateful.

Some of these prose poems were initially read at the New Cadence Poetry Series in Santa Cruz, Ca.

Cover design by Sansmaya.

Table of Contents

Parataxis:

1a: coordinate ranging of clauses, phrases, or words one after another without coordinating connectives – 1b: the placing of a subordinate clause beside a main clause without a subordinating connective –

2: the parataxic mode of experience

PARATAXIS

Too Early

Strains sift softly through an early rising – On a deserted street remains the light a painter inadvertently left behind – Under this marled sky, the link between worlds reconfigures – Distant roads become everyday streets, the years get logged as miles – Just the act of walking segues to a motion of jeopardy, a syntax waiting out any return to balance – A voluptuous vulnerability no longer distracts – As trembling strength fosters the day's questionable events, I realize I finally own myself ...

Any talk of premature withdrawal disavows an appetite for risk, which by current standards is clearly obsessional – Attachments to illusion's continuance provide I-know-not-what comforts to the chained and weary, the carbon-based menaces still terrorizing the neighborhoods – Through the armpits of embrangled mornings, the single focus homeboys drive their chariots, their destination the headwaters of my daily reckoning ...

Tough Little World

These mornings cripple me with endless possibility – Freedom to move freedom to stay – To choose or not – Like Damascus steel, both equally fatal – As the weather gets hotter, the cracks increase – All this talk of looming revolution affects the genesis of my breathing – Some days just leave one feeling strangled bludgeoned and dumped by the side of the road – But with my need to make a difference, I get myself back up, brush it off and head back for more – In this somber summer, all the narrow spaces seem to be, or are, looming large ...

I covet the manna of anxious work, to rise from the ashen lethargy of my contradicted hours – I go with adapting what's usable and discard the rest, even if it has to be dismantled first – Particulars are the fragments that goad, that by which complacent shadows are toppled – As the metaphysical epistemologist, the one with rheumy eyes full of impending death, sadly informed me: it sure does get brutal in this tough little world ...

Big Picture

The human soul, fetus of silly putty that it is, has impressionable edges expanding contracting in ratios of perilous creation, it's all there in the ineffable small print if anyone wants to bother taking it in, evolutionary process is an experimental heat sink in this sky engulfed world ...

Convulsions of the absurd glue together this swirling spectacle of dust and dissonance – One little orb spinning away in a wilderness of sparks – Even as the hermetic enigma was around long before the winged messenger came on the scene – The long sought after particle, once observed, will not likely evaporate the pervasive mysteries either – Hints of Orpheus will yet echo down from the heights as cultural savages will insist on migrating through the gates of modern barbarism ...

A Prevailing Instinct

Upon arising from my bed of dust, mumbling in front of the mirror becomes the first item of morning protocol – With an existence-in-ruins, I wipe up remnants of the previous night's intransigent overflows – Even in the Church of the Daily Deal, where worship whispers through the daily slaughter, a dodging of pub darts, seasonal bird droppings, and BBQ embalmed animal parts is done with panache and wholly inadequate focus, straight-up illusions bolstering my instincts for further preservation ...

In this strange & unique life, currently there's way too much white space white noise white rice – Can you blame a guy for oversleeping when he gets the chance? – Then again, any forward motion decrees fortitude even as comedy yet sucks on the tit of tragedy – Endlessly, these hours should, and will continue to be, randomly engineered ...

Phantoms Conversing

I drive north through the grandiose gestures of the dirt merchants, the Big Men who shelter their monsters in back rooms – I am the road sailor navigating the shoals of contracting life, salubrious days no longer bothering to work out the contingencies, the neon blaze of all this screaming irony no longer even *feeling* affordable ...

The vociferating infatuants rail on, the radio speaker pulsing with the savage syllables, these proclaimed artifices devoid of any scripted scruples, my vagrant sympathies murderous at times, survival now a singular obsession, the waking hours seized as insurance against any more dubious weather and/or rigorous indiscretion ...

An unforeseen event, now before me a former love passes – We amazingly exchange words in the vatic fragments of phantoms conversing ...

Outlasting the Ninnies

No question, she has pre-determinant instincts for personal catastrophe – In the particular majesty of the particular, she keeps draping her melancholic wreckage across and over my unwilling semblance – The furor of her light yet swells the flesh, the rigor of her *morte* smiles on through her set of cracked incisors ...

Whatever O – I sign off on the raw surprises that await, I gnaw upon the savage bones of impermanence – It truly is OK that these ill-fitting hours continue to dodge the taxman – Sustained by alleged reprieve, what remains is an offering guaranteed to provoke the longest silence – False mercy should not and will not be an issue this time around ...

Deal with It

Under the beam of antlers, we hold the pose until satiated – Once there was whisky; yet it too yielded to the days of obligation – Blown out on the perimeter, sounds of acrimony fade to just angry fatigue – Times such as these suggest that I sleep with my head towards Mecca and dwell in the light of blasphemy – The neighboring sky is all I need to grind out auguries of edged tool precision – Self love comes crashing in as I stagger through the white knuckled afternoons – My only need in this undeclared moment just might hinge upon the right mix of oils ...

The day remains a contract full of questionable ink – I mean, how exciting can lassitude actually be? – Even with the whippin' post days long left in the dust, these preferred methods of auto-destruction, as inexorable as Alexander rolling along with his armies through Persia, do remain in bounds and in play ...

And yet, as the fetchings fail to appear, I default to indiscriminate borrowings – Apropos of nothing palpable, I plead with unknown forces: please kick me down some daily bread ...

First Impression

That last chance I ever had was half an hour in on this road to nowhere – But now the daily deal is just contention amidst the howling integers, my visage remaining subject to further bleed out – So great is the slippage of moments, I fail to log these increments fast enough – Since apprecia-tions can be embedded in just about anything, please now welcome my grim grace ...

Any attempt at making futurity bulletproof just might leave your throat exposed – Fragments of this world, glued together with research powered by the scans, may sustain any future activity, even as some captured solace would be real good right about now ...

Wake me when it's over

For openers, we have proverbial insomnias determined not to incubate in the sanctimonious, nay stupefying, headlines soon to be de-commissioned by these heroes lounging away in the rosy ruins – Let us preserve something to mitigate the bastardnomics, now insurging our future forfeited – The plan is to just give 'em enough rope so they can finish the job ...

Fiery apparitions perform a first act, long over before it even begins – Why is this political pissing match contingent upon such enormous bladders and little dicks? – Household deities aren't going to be much help, especially when you're fooling around with these incendiary micronovas ...

Still, I await for any of this to make some sense – Any response on my part may involve a series of interlocking sighs of circumstance, which most likely would be equivalent to a plethora of scenarios yet to eventuate – The apprenticeship in underwriting any of these strange events may then cross the uncrossable, the outcome only another rapture default ...

Live

It's only curtains if you fail to believe in something – To get on with the "hang" of living, it helps to put some effort into parody – Like sidestepping the toxic terrors of Martha Stewart's take on modern living – And certainly it's a good idea never to piss off the people who handle your food – All of these plastic implements have recently tried going indigenous and have failed spectacularly – Nature just doesn't do the "aw shucks" thing ...

"A hesitant assertion is not an assertion of hesitation" may be indicative of more elitist slobbering, while the fringe of stunned citizenry remains in vastly vulnerable mode ...

The practitioners of brute torque, of angular body posings, the thrallers of the heal: all of them now fraughtly wondering what's up with the lost/last leavings ...

Self's Pursuit

Since he looks like himself, he should be easy to spot – As embolisms of inertia had rapidly began to decoagulate, he had hastily thrown the scraps of love onto the midnite hour and just began walking walking walking – His franchise of inaccuracy had never been much of a viable option anyway – Some of the locals even conjectured as to whether the malaise resulted from too much Ovaltine, or was perhaps just the result of messy standards ...

However, when integrity is at stake, catharsis sure beats sitting around – As in: aren't ethical dilemmas *always* time sensitive? – Like if one's style of gestures becomes a signature unique to each gesticulator, then languid motions in the still afternoons are all that really needs to be accomplished – How else might we account for life's tenuously valid haulout on the shores of this pale spinning speck ...?

Finest Hour

My lover's voice is the kissing wind, the one in which betrayal goes alurking –
Wearing the perfume of a mad mystic, her dreams penetrate mine – Intimacy
thus remains the chapter you write when stuck in solitary – Interior
penumbras marginally light the necessities, *feeling* all that counts in these
ticking hours ...

Bouquets of the marvelous summon caresses like butterfly breath –
Wondering: how did it all get started with that distanced thank you? – Love
now out- lives this opaque evening sky, full of such serious lucidity – These
framed moments attempt to translate her cryptic smile as I utter: My god, the
horrible brilliance of it all ...

Legacy

My hard drinking forebears, potent beings that they were, apparently let the holdings slip away – Four large cattle ranches lost to the whiskey bottle and bad marriage – Perhaps that loss today would be attributable via too much color TV – Oh well, now in the silt of ancestors, the deal is that some of the descendants are "in film" and most definitely hating life – In this laboratory of social chaos called California, the inflamed tissues of ingratitude keep certifying banality across the seared and acrid landscapes ...

If anything, it's the winning of trophies that's holding us back – Deluded Man fleeing Modern Man – A pyre of assumptions just bringing on more petty failure – Really wondering where that "anti-pathos" inoculation is when we feverishly need it most ...?

Soapbox

People talk of the human situation like it was something deserving of its own question mark – What is this, some weird badly timed joke, an appalling deceit carnival? – The half dead soldiers are returning from the devouring theatre, their mothers having to feed them by hand yet once again ...

To delete/squelch the republic's hijackers, this should be the first imperative – Stealth scenarios such as "trans-parent diplomacy" just add more oxymorons to the list – It seems that when people who have never been soldiers make the wars, then the graffiti of doom will yet kneel before us ...

Defrag

In an exile of promise, in the isness of nothing, I invent sweeping preoccupations – The hell with the polemics, it's the treasure of daily chaos that cancels out the world's loathing – Each befuddled moment a seed crystal unpacking the glaring the daring the outrageous acts of this temporal stay – And yes, it is laughter that always works as the most brazen eraser of misfortune and folly ...

On this sphere where the Vulgarati gibber on, senselessly disturbing the ether, the noise of mere words ceaselessly fills the afternoon voids – Here, cattywompus is actually a form of dork ballet – In defrag mode, I no longer need to hold a candle to the mattering brightness – The edges of my presence dissolve into a despairing focus as I observe that horn o' plenty, the one we've all taken for granted, and yes, the very same one that is now quite empty ...

Position Statement

On the other side of summer is September, can't wait for that relief, and vertigo, I mean heart-seizing vertigo, is as close to coagulated disembodiment as one can get – In the clarity of that raw rare moment (is this what they mean by eternity?), the cooling afternoon breezes fill me with marginal hope, even a brief respite from the inane ravings of the 40 oz. philosophers ...

What we call blue happens to be my favorite atmospheric secretion – Daylight promises all when you live out in the combustible woods – The beginning of each day bodes nullity, grief, and utmost opportunity – My core need is only to remain barefoot along the trails of each day's profane adventuring – That outside world I detect is uncannily the same one reflected from within ...

Justine

I have a girlfriend in Paris whom I have yet to meet – Absence has never been so fluent, or language so mute – Yet, her avidities bring on the chance minglings of innocence and guile – When I touch the go-button, that now-under-wraps turbine fire shall commence – A crimson ripening will alloy to the late hours – We will swim through the warring deserts, our seizures will become the genesis of further clarity – Perhaps then the rooftops of Europe will sanction the defenestrations of our love ...

Right now, it could be raining in her garden for all I know – She could be drowning in smoke as she intones my name – Her enunciations might be flattening out the vowels as her candor buzzes behind those winking eyes – In the invincible darkness, she will dissolve and kneel before the shadows of martyrs – In her molecular passion, she prays to incorporate me into a wound of monstrous hunger – It will be then that we shall arrive, at that appropriate moment, wondering if we are there yet ...

Fluxus

On the night breath express, my return to the trembling dust becomes re-certified – Holding out for incremental improvements, poverty always the whetstone upon which my incisors have become sharpened – Balance is now hunkered down and just waiting it out – I swim on as my surroundings all go up in smoke ...

Entrails, tattoos, salt grains . . . all dissolved between the rhythms of bone and stone – In the act of walking is my blood altered, are my tools honed – These night breaths are carried around in my left hip pocket, salvation a process not a state – To achieve the imperfect is all that's being asked for ...

The Bird is a Word

Here at Nepenthe, the condor cruising by conquers my vision – Such an awesome visual, more suprising than if Johnny Quest had just gone gliding past on his Roc – The sublimity of the condor's yard long primaries holding the wind, barely a movement of those wings – This majestic creature sweeps on to the north, my gaping semblance stunned with awe ...

Words and birds, both carriers of premonitions and the initiatives of lightning, invested with trance prospects over against the mundane adventures of men, both defying gravity's hold – To behold this spirit frontier triggers this sway over and through inexorable life ...

This weekend's trip south has been a rejuvenating pause, a link-up over the astral waves with Hermes on his fifth millennial birthday – The concern now is how to return to the dreadful sphere – Shrugging, I raise my glass and drink to the totemic wisdoms ...

Just the Visuals

Losing the dreams as opposed to rejecting them – This prolific emptiness endlessly reproducing itself - Like the mingling of shadows, like the discredit of wayward angels – As you are tempted to requisition the inaccessible, plunder some imagery along the way – Grab a vision as antidote for the poisonous stupors – Truly I wish only to know how one mounts the daily charades while whistling darkly ...

Nothing like a walk in the clouds to revive all those childhood memories and despairs – Some would say it's all turbulent, all love and strife – Myself, I return to various apertures of the past, futilely retracing the fading glyphs – Not knowing what might possibly be looked for, I focus on astonishing events soon to occur ...

Just Wondering

This realm beyond language, like oh yes your ass is perfect, like the swinging motion of hammocks – Some would say poetry, while others might infer the hoarding of attentions – Auguries from reassembled fragments, random generation indicated, no returns necessary – Seerages done with tongue-upon-nipple, she is positioned well under the trance wall, her precision movements languid and luminous somewhere west of the moon ...

The unspoken, now getting written, written up against the crumbling disharmonies, a word like "kingdom" given a new meaning in the grip of the dead and the dread, certainty in foreclosure and likely to stay that way, whiffed by the putrid aromas of decline, and yet who now, please tell me, is to play-act the role of Noxious Queen ...?

Hold It

I barter for more western days, journeys to far places achieved vicariously, the strange maladies become more familiar, the next door misanthropes become more dug in, no, there is nothing yielding about my present aspect ...

Azure evenings are my current religion, while personal experience is like a lost traipse through unknown forests – I saunter through the Taco Twilight, thirty years removed from all I ever missed – Past performances were usually a matter of unwanted palpitations anyway – Since the unexpected is always incoming, I ask only to be buried face down in my ashes, a final enactment done under the sky's watery intent ...

Long Shot

Irritation serves many purposes, such as ignoring the Big Man as he swaggers past groping his dangling hindrance – If the wear and tear don't take you down, perhaps it might be the corporate dogmas that do you in – Likewise, when you're down to your last silver dollar ... now that's real duress – At that point, it's time to get out the jousting sticks and charge through the ranks of the Venerable Ninnies – Yes, that is right, just for the privilege of staying clean and reasonably alive ...

Of course, it's these hazy results that I am fully responsible for – My grip has yet to slip however, even as all my drive-bys involve the targeting of digits with ammoless ejaculations – Espying a curvy prospect, I give her the trice-over – She returns the stare, comes over and gets right in my face, demanding "Will you work for your love ...?"

Beyond, the burning

The terrain is burning in wind whipped fury this morning – The chaparral's just doing what it's done for millions of years, long before the silly people arrived and got in the way – The only so-called tragic part is all this arrogant cluelessness ...

Backwinds gusting through the opulent privations, hard to tell what's been trampled and what remains intact – Our inhabitations are postponed, the neglected spaces duly evacuated – Because smoke jolts the breath, the sky is wild and opaque – This neighboring mountain has disappeared into the fury of a half-century burn – After this inferno, the hot rocks will return to the cooling air – That is, only after the wind decides who gets nailed ...

These furious fires full-tilt should assassinate any further complacency – Trying to buck the evidence, that should fuck you up all the more – As I shelter up in the intervals, the weight of dawn lodges somewhere between my ears – The charge-offs of this burning world only point out the necessary flee directions – Untouched by flame, yet consumed by consequence, it is your distant proximity which now recedes along with the fire wind ...

As this forest burns, an ancient bird prepares for rising – Smoke and fog combine alchemically in the Paleolithic evening, loosening up the knot of dusk, the crepuscular lode – One more sunrise has yet been delayed as we await the vegetation's return ...

Bushwacker

Mad money debouched from pockets not my own, by default I fall back upon the currency of spit – As I stagger on, the vultures circle with increasing levels of interest – My sweating heart is barely able to contain all this tangential evidence – With heatstroke looming, my quaking legs rise to meet the incline, my thirst the newly unforeseen situation ...

I marvel at the trajectories of instinct-perfected raptors, at the blue blossoms filling the air with exuberance – Appreciations of life reach a new peak as this inexorable exposure points towards an odds-on oblivion – And to think that my family right now is still wondering what I do for a living ...

The Meaning of Success

Nasty looks to match the stiletto heels, a dancing straight from her guts –
Feasting upon the loaves of paradise, her brusque hands drunk with fun, my
observations available for rent to any and all interested parties – O yes
tapestry of wayward night, what could possibly be left to exalt? – And what is
this, an ambient noise in our eyes' intercourse? – How can I garner more
kisses when I'm flinching at memories of those last savage ones ...?

If this was a movie shot, no doubt I'd be crawling back with gusto to the
absent prior – However, the raw reality of it now stands: My lips parched, this
life swamped with undulation, I manage to get vertical and gasp: YES I AM
BROKE ...

Not Quite Futile

Sitting around watching my inbox, surely there are more compelling things to be done – A believer in disbelief as I am, only an appreciation of the Unreal can suggest what all this mortal straining is about – Through the soup of dissonance, mediocrity tends to breed its own equations – In this savage world, apparently the infantile-minded still win out, history only illustrating that which is yet to be forgotten – And all this cursing of not-quite-futile ghosts, now what does that accomplish ...?

More immediate than the illumination of wanderers is this wrestling match with life every day – The local empties and cigarette butts along the road greet my swollen eyes each morning, hinting at further subjection to all sorts of mundane insult – It takes all I've got just to keep from slapping myself – Folly still hangs from its plastic crucifix, acquired stupidities keep choking right along – Reflected in this weary gaze, here comes yet another uninvited messiah on the rising winds ...

Sojourner

Like those others, the invisible ones, we arrived on the Exile Express from somewhere east of the Pleiades – Our upraised digits indicate this as being so – Remaining in deep cloister mode, we remain prisoners of the Infinite – Thus, our survival is assured – Tomorrow somehow becomes the furniture we sit upon today ...

Dream deities move the morning, salty words move the poem, the sperm auditors evoke the rot that feeds upon blood's glimmer, to love is to destroy disillusionment silence all the rest – And if that's not sufficient, the high tide that night directs will be sweeping it all back out to the big water very very soon ...

Ur Gnomics

Isn't it Unreason that the philosophers can't hack? – Yet bring up the subject of Nothingness, and it all turns into a feeding frenzy – The disputing gets all tangled up in which came first, life or ontology – You mean to tell me that knowledge is only accessible when the lights are left on? – If a sequence of words may, or may not, become a sentence, then the value of anything must be beyond language – This leads to thinking that rationality is an acquired disease that only produces further ignorance ...

Since the philosophers are never satisfied, what is called philosophy might itself be pathological – That horizon out there may be an illusion, but the unexpected surely brightens what hours remain – Breath, soul, fire ... I mean, how can one even dispute that guy Heraclitus ...?

Still Breathing

Next to dogged resolve, the sempiternal was the mantic gesture that decreed me back to life, each forward motion a reprieve of sorts, the ground of light dialoguing with spit in the mind free hours, philosophical questions striving to span the spin, signals from the other worlds determined to break in through the tinnitus, the distant spheres and hyper-sensory music downloaded via alchemy's regenesis, every goodbye becoming a paraphrase of summoning ...

Since I dwell in the invasive habitats, getting lost is daily accomplished with fervor – As invitations to create embody further desire, intrepid beings I accost usually put some teeth into my judgments – That place called Eden, meanwhile, will always remain a conjecture ...

Deterrence

Curating the unseen under the influence of symbolic elegy, the insomnia serpent in her midnite nest vexes sleep's composure, any dream a far reach, her vigils sustained by continuous turnings – Semi-castratos as myself expect the non-existent work to keep flooding the impoverishment, while this walk upon thorns suggests that I should aggressively brandish a vulgar digit at the passing drone spectacles ...

Starving on the crumbs of jaded largesse, the arrogant moralists drink down their affluenzas, their not-so-private glories – I disavow these people, instead acting out an ascetic lifestyle worthy of St. Anthony – My dogged presence should be enough to deter the executioner, mostly because I'm just too damn ornery to die ...

Futility on Purpose

Who is doing the talking here, always a matter of dispute, the antiphilosophers still in the saddle riding hard, the Marlboro Man swathed in counterfeit smoke, "Gittin' old ain't for sissies" he mumbles around a dangling cigarette (rolled), the prisoners of net price are casting off the itching questions while the Unknown eventually solves everything, these Roadrunner reruns sure help out in the shuffle of my purposeful futility ...

This ink dries before it hits the paper – The rustlings of this creaking memory, like winds full of ash and embers – Disturbance is the constitution of the world, destiny not something that submits readily to secret knowledge – In other words, this daily existence has to either equal or surpass itself ...

Run Time Error

Verbal combat seems strictly for adroit idiots, I don't care how suave your dark limpidity may be – In the background I hear Freddie Mercury trying to hit the high notes, sounding like some freshly neutered midget – Boogie, Bugalu, break it down, whatever, at least my soundtracks still provide a royalty stream, what the hell ...

If I could just reverse-engineer the darkness so that the downtimes aren't so gruesome, then a fresh myth of being-this-guy might emerge – Destruction's just the dark side of creation anyway, am I wrong? – So, with this in mind, aren't we all asking ourselves just how the future will likely contour around these current abandonments? – Verily, it is not enough that the apricot orchards are inexcusably neglected while ambrosia salad still gets served up at Grandma's place every Sunday afternoon ...

Shut Up and Eat

Pundits feeding the corruption mixer, crapulous moments in the prophecy depot, all the dead off someplace just shaking their heads in disgust, these spit zones of teenage angst and tears ripple along with dull reproach - Certainly this is when fried potatoes make the morning, all else volun-teering for the forsaken ...

Like Jesus riding in on his donkey, making it pretty damn clear he's nobody's messiah, I lurk and loom with the embittered felons, missing out on all those photo-ops with the beautiful people – In these inhabited moments of fire & ice, loitering is an accomplished dream, from spark to smolder – Love hesitates yet moves in the afternoon as the work goes undone – I wear this necklace of staggered night as an accomplished insomniac might possibly display ...

Remedy

The rising of the suffering sons, borne through parental indifference, all beyond ministrations of the stone healers, the task of gestures goes crashing through the whistling rhetorics, only the aroma of grace shields the lost ones now from the greed driven terra-trovers ...

Sure my spleen gets bent with the anti-social careers of these retards – These ill feelings will most likely defer my bodhisattva nomination (yawn) – Also, this flagging vitality will sure as hell make for some more personal danger events ...

Some have their plastic crucifixes to fall back on – Me, I just beat the drum of less red meat – News from the various wastelands, when it arrives, is just pre-history with too many modern twists ...

Wagering on Illusion

Since we are all born of integrated elements, malformation likely points to an embrangled heritage – Our kluged minds bumble along in daily disorder, indicating a who-knows-what end – Some think by referencing Aristotle, solutions may be imminent – More appropriate might be Xenophon's take on what Socrates was about ...

In my iridescent nightmares, in my biochemical ballets, magic turns to physics in a captive atmosphere that verily crawls through these impossible nights – The bite of poverty on brooding flesh, a non-exempt mind tangled up in conundrum – It seems existence can only default to her own reclining hips, the ones that advertise YES – Each inhalation, of course, is the clarion by which her bones become burnished – By way of her acrid diction, we are the chosen ones stricken with omnipresent liberty – Oh yes rampant illusion, our surprises shall be aligned and furthered ...

Buzz On

This burning wind never fails the collateral reaches, even when the audio is switched off – Like when things are going great, don't you just want to punch it into overdrive? – In a world where aptitude goes disguised as public humiliation, where we're all indexed to the secular, it is these reprieves which are always full priced – The good times reach for, pell-mell and willy-nilly, the defiantly obvious, the wingnut agendas continuing to confound …

Once I was viable; but endeavor has now been reduced to pulling on the ear lobes – Don't recall if amnesia was part of my service contract or not, but the proclivity to dawdle certainly is – And if I had any nerves right now, believe me, you'd be on them – Really, I do not have a clue as to what might be consequential anymore – In this standby mode, not too much it seems …

Rework

Insolent skies contribute to a deepening joy, fateful days look askance at the murder of stones – In everyday's flux, the eyes assemble various degrees of the unseen, a trust in primitive chemistry encouraging raw prosperity – To see past the bleeding past the lies, deep involvements indicated, cloud reverie in pathways as timing is everything, the goading-on like bare feet on hot asphalt, all this is promised if only to ingest more light and blink past the bitter parts – Emptiness yet remains something suggestive of ...

A Few Regrets

These daffodils, ready to bust open just as I'm starting to shut down – On sunny days, I formerly experienced the poetry of impairments – When touched, I became demagne-tized, solitude then defaulted as my pushbutton opiate – Driven by memory's shrapnel, I now ask: Is remorse ever *not* bleak ...?

The returning sun undoes this mummy wrap of winter – The shining of druthers gets into position, the retreat into lessness ready to stage the hormonal resurrection – Where need delimits new creations, the sling-slang usually tries sneaking back in through the cat door – Any respite in this epoch not a question of if but of when ...

Strikeout

This afternoon, the sun continues to bleed the way a stone captures smoke –
My heart, reconciled to your akimbo stance, beats along with the fire in your
hair – My charm now in tatters, I may as well finish off the goal of achieving
maximum opacity – I ask her if she is still in the groove – She slyly slurs
around her wink, "Naw, just pretending ..."

At a later time, there might be the merge of hand and breast, a dagger of allure
deftly poised – Briefly we might be as hungry as Melville's cannibals, our
prayers composed of wide-eyed sweating – In the search for a puzzle to go
with this missing piece, everything demands the torching of this wayward
flesh ...

The Sound of Light

Forgetfulness usually sets in right after sundown – Has something to do with getting situated toward the future tense – Might this not be analogous to the way time decomposes as it heightens the profane moments? – Sure it's tempting to think it may all be over, but the petty furors indicate otherwise – By using desultory verbiage, I now seek to outlast the frozen spots in this heart of mine – Perhaps an assault on the inevitable will underwrite further longevity ...

Meanwhile, the sound of light turns the aforementioned accretions into a much bigger ash heap than the flames of love never quite anticipated – This because time's drool has always been a family favorite – We're talking a plethora of insignificance as this body, designed for so much wear and tear, soldiers on through the wounding thickets – Holding back on the charm acrobatics, I duly tilt on in the lizard populated afternoons ...

Shaker Weather

Survival on the faultline now pays my dues – Outside in wayward juxtapose, a contrail intersects the mare's tails in a burgeoning spring sky – This territory has always been a jigsaw, a geography on rations, presupposed by outlines of the invisible world ...

Weather pleasure, a portal to the Marvelous: there are still places here where you can abscond with your beloved – Places of clean air and scattered light beckon to a rendezvous in forgotten locales – These steadfast oak temples, the havens of solace – By the scansion of earth and sky, this amazing place can only be about the trans-parencies of gods ...

The Marvelous

Nothing comes close to perfection like the lips of Athena, myth being proportionate to what? – Vectors of Orpheus call out for further ekstasis – As the higher magics diffuse, revelations happen in the intervals, the proof embedded in new forms emerging ...

Portents of soothsayers scribed upon their murmuring altars – Their tranced testimonies resonate in hermetic gold, divining the limits of con-fusions as the words become uttered – Birds awaken prophecy in their restless motions, a randomweave living in preservations of smoke ...

I rub my eyes endlessly as intuition signals distant events in far space – The synaptic leaps still boggle, while sudden smiles remain the best of investments – For the modern primitive, the mind yet provides a notebook for the Marvelous ...

No Sabe Nada

Eschewing the viable, all endeavor becomes the least common denominator in the research for precarious symbols – Like the masks of intent, like starving maneuvers, the psyche aches for accomplished contradiction ...

Interesting, this idea that there can be planned hallucinations – Followed by the idea that I had best use this notion – Otherwise, there could be a sharp down climb through untenable personas – Taking the muse by the throat, in desperate acts of scrounging up some material, has sometimes been the only option open – It tends to be more pragmatic than philosophical voodoo putting on some persuasion offensive ...

Still, I believe it all comes down to the immortality problematic – Set upon the flanks of ruin, what medley of bewitchments might still ensue here? – Like hyperbola distended in plagues of further quantum flatulence, I do believe we are talking some serious nada ...

Allegory for What ...?

My adventures have known limits, the current oracle remains in rags, and this disfigured flesh trails honesty as I hip-hop over whatever the fuck is ailing me in this humid hour – Spontaneity breathes all around, the blessed wind enacts its own declarations – Thoughts circle, this living always subject to condensations – Breathing death though various wounds, I crawl back to a prior life – Takes all I've got not to keep kicking my backside ...

What is that hot rush in the foreground of these earthly tremors? – Who cares, the tears will still get shed without noticible weeping – Walking the highways, time just a thrown switch clicking off this trance pace – Maybe it's only the geometries of the damned that indicate when one's number comes up – Meanwhile, vertigo tends to be an allegory for what ...?

Awake

When fate gets stale and dark, maybe it's time to change the angles – My form emerges at noon, aberration planning to call for some shots – Episodes of the unexpected just whack you into immediate attention some days – As my hands plot offset devolutions, these scrappy knuckles favor the bar's neon oasis – Later, those same shots involved a blur default, it becoming apparent that the lapdancer had made off with the guy's cell phone – Simply put, she was nimble as monk smoke – He could only let go with a resigned "It's all yours babe ..."

In her absence we returned to the trickle juice, set and ready to grapple with the impermanent remains of the evening, the dog days determined to underwrite the necessary staggers – Outside, the clouds huddled up, indifferent to our vain seizures of manliness ...

Gender Sync

Her touch could slay a legion – The kind of leap only a saint might have intimacy with – Afternoons built on love, the measure of her jewel, auguries performed against her sovereign breasts, beckoning towards the final floral decree – A butterfly tattooed upon her sacrum, she triangulates further incorporation – Genuinely am I baffled how four billion years of DNA flux has led to this ...

At the intersection of these stars is a pendulum that never swings, romantic weekends on the Strip be damned – As I step in and out of post-coital reconstitution, the haulout of lusty embers has never been so questionable ...

This Epoch

This epoch just about over as the tribes of tiny things make and do not make our actions possible – Under the turmoil and controversies, contentment still feels like a shakedown – Until joy returns, weeping will yet be on hold – Wondering: just how much snake oil must we ingest from the experts and transparent diplomats before we examine and reorient? – And Scripture, my friends, will be no help on this one either ...

Tolerance and/or attempted tact might open otherwise locked doors – But didn't that guy from Nazareth mingle with the temple harlots? – Oh yeah, that really pissed the enforcers off – Got the crucifixion dudes mobilized in a hurry on that one ...

These soothsayer presagements etched in the prescient air, the sky never pretending never needing to – Time slipping past as all tends to the forgiven flow – Near and distant creatures will know not of our passions as drunken men rummage for their runcible redemptions – Fate closes in on some much quicker than for those of us left behind ...

Last Days

Bulldogging through invincible moments, echoes pass right through me, weeping, laughing, it doesn't matter, side-stepping the toxic chitchats, my pervasive blind spot the self-gift that keeps on giving, poetry is a strategy not a game, can't remember the last time I actually felt trans-lucent, the deception of landscapes still resonates well, hyperbole the sine qua non the meat & potatoes of all who captivate the chronically gullible such as I, shake-the-booty still the orphan of desire, saxophone widows palm the terse memories, the mindless to & fros devoid of motion, the night crews busy with fetish abatement, shadows swarm in our nothing retentions as we run down the avenues, arms folded in the last days of life of death, motions of hope fall into evening's demise as her fingers pierce me with demonic tenderness, this abdominal flinching of mine only confirming where the knife first went in ...

A Rarity of One

Rarely do I pick it up and get it down right the first time – Precision escapes me with its anointments, the way cerulean blue knocks me right out – Regardless of the infinite stupidities measured out, this spinning little orb will persist – It's a wonder our feet still carry us, even as everything points to other worlds – I mean, how can you keep your eyes on the road when there's a precipice up ahead ...?

Anyway, all this fear about waiting only reveals anxiety re: tomorrow's conjectured demise – The return of the primitive will as yet undercut the modern conceits – Huddled up against the barbarity of this rimless world, our trembling lives still get dusted with the cherry blossoms, which uncannily have arrived early this year ...

Pilgrim

A traveler with no passport, no baggage, no destination, I curve and traipse with the seasons – A series of departures with endlessly deferred arrivals – Movements are mostly forward strokes – I continue to push this empty wheelbarrow through the portals of eternity, subject to plenty of loitering at the rest stops of course ...

Waiting is redeemed when the past turns up in brackets, when the piling of clouds and weather incantations scribe out an evolutionary path, that which drove Ulysses forward with the beguiling nymphs and geometrical peregrinations – As in these invisible walkabouts of my own need, danger is always in the allure that lurks ...

Such is a question: Why may I not live like I wish to breathe, deeply and without resistance? – To reach for what remains starkly in front of you, then might equilibrium be satisfyingly blind – And really, I remain a stranger as to whether any of this can be usefully assimilated ...

Where I'm At

Agreeably, preoccupations with calamity have been deleted – My daily tightrope walk over the abyss nothing more than the gestation of reprieves – Through a series of half-deaths, even pleasure is nourished in its evanescence ...

Arms akimbo before the human window, the one I stare out twenty five hours a day, each viewing a crucial experiment reserved for the non-ordinary carnage of apparitions – Muzzling the negginators has not been as effective as siphoning off their gas, their identities hung out on the line like laundry adornments – As a second nature, this poverty and the sharpening of knives have always served me well ...

Mystery's Sweepout

Furious beauty greets these opening eyes – The mountains will remain indifferent, the ceaseless water never resting, shadows of unknown days emerge by bird divinations ...

Red sky, blue water: we exist as carbonized forms where dark patterns dwell – In one sense, it's all mutating, gnosis underpinning the ramified future, service to others being the rent paid for this residency ...

Cloud breath like love leaking through the sieve of providence, even as my judgments never extend to the evening skies – These echoes of Urania and the beauty of agates proof enough to defy the naysayers ...

Chops & Licks

This weariness, a reality-fatigue, the by-product of so much high octane hassle – Any respite confounds while it also frees up – A healthy respect for gravity remains this primary change agent – Mortality strains along as vigilance iotas foster more tenuous survival – A succession of opaque noons blur into one big fat now-moment, an inflection point that must be in space yet isn't ...

Endurance attempts to negate the theatricals and the mindless tyrannies – By such, the imagined determines how to transcend the known – On this kitchen table, portents appear in the spilled salt, a granular chaos that bears witness to prior designs – Having said farewell to the drudge work long ago, only then could the work of the image be remade – It was when the debits fully erased the credits that starting over beat any further ass-dragging ...

Licentia Vatum

Metaphor as anti-empirical solvent – True idioms cast off on a windy syntax, tragedy's various tumults in luminous imagining, poesis really only accomplished by the outlaws, bold leapings through opal fire clouds, an occasional nod from a guest oracle looking over the impurities, how is it that the blinders of commerce delude/preclude the poet's task-creations ...?

The poet from the north took to writing his poems upon tree bark, a gnosis inscribed for the initiates – In words with intangible value, that gold cache of the rainbow known as Apollinaire, hardwired by his muse, his imagination working through the trepanned skull, yet lucid through to the feverish end, spoke from the heart of zone as the unmetaphors got poetically transformed ...

Orpheus in endless loop, poetry rises on painfully ardent thermals – The poet continues to guard an endangered metabolism, intrepidly, before a breath is even taken ...

Scattershot

Anabasis sputters along over the apocalyptic cracks, the profanely sacred drifting through the smoky mornings, this crow-loving wind knifes through these rasping hands – On remote beaches, the foretellers lie with their thirsty fragments, hydro-alchemy now the current gold standard, needing a sync-job with respiration are the prayers at the heart of the world, songs of exile still burn upon her singed lips, time's myopia nails us all in thematics of absence presence and overall nonsense ...

This one percent of the world's perceivable reality tends to mere scattershot for the cinematic eye – The high tech magics resound with the ancient prescripts, pundits of no-thing-ness attempt to abstract the mute facts *sotto voce* – And yet, without these ancestral secrets remaining unfurl-ed, the world will not move on in further ellipsis ...

Better than Color TV

Diamonds of the Seven Sisters dance above in the deep winter night – Glyphs of the immortals remain in unknown code – I grow old attempting to clinch the Now under the hum of far paradise – The fading edges of the Milky Way will be an eventual destination ...

The sky the sky ... the sky that sanctions the great circles, the one that girds the pillaged landscapes below – The local fire stones lie coarse and cracked in time's womb – This because I must reside in this wilderness for the sheer beckoning of these ancient lights ...

Road Trip

Under the sun's fatal beneficence, I drive through strange towns wondering about my freak-of-nature status – All those dismissed messages from childhood, dismissed only because of the baggage factor – Like a meteor roaring through a cold sky, I continue in purposeful trajectory – The work shall resume in precipitating mode, the results will flow through gutters both precarious and functional ...

Shrouded in the comings and goings of tenuous account-ability, my life a roulette wheel spinning with impossible-to-read numbers – Just forcing these eyelids open every morning becomes an act of unrivaled accomplishment ...

Parts Unknown

Leggy women working the streets, summoning fictions and possibly some piasters, no girdles for these midriffs, the craving for uppers driving *that* horse downtown, voluptuous and pale flesh in dumb display, the covert combat of gender events vaguely foreshadowed – In spite of the bump and grind follies, these days clearly will not be in vain ...

The tavern maidens keep pouring forgetfulness in endless motions, sun fetishes prevail in the rattling darkness – Mornings are exempt from our little troubles, the unhinged power-trippers quivering & quavering past their former grandiosities, their accumulated love of ecological treason and the bric-a-brac imponderables now lying aground in the wastelands – The bathetic force that built all the suburbs has now moved on to other gaping wonders ...

Madness and Dogs

A chorus of temporal retellings is all I've got left – An ad hoc raving a writing over told perhaps – The misdirected lives of others have always been my lifelong study, useful just enough to induce a desultory traipse through plucky days – These indigenous weathers sure do rumple my cover however, just as madness dogs my shining wounds – Sure there's plenty to mutter about – The sole option left is to toot like hell and wail on in the passing air ...

This desired loss now becomes someone else's dangerous gain – Like courteous relations all covered with bloody fingerprints, it really does seem like the experts in having fun are the very ones now responsible for killing us off – Yes, humor *is* a serious business – But how does that justify any promoted distinction between happy and grim flowers? – The dancing only seems to get crazier as the lessons get rougher – Demonstrating this healthy cynicism is my sanctioned drawing right against any further loss of consciousness ...

Goofball

Ho! – I run down the street, balancing a full bottle of coke upon my pointy head, the lights suddenly fade as I encounter something very hard – A Good Samaritan type pulls me out of the bushes – But instead of pieces of silver, he offers me a show-stopping snarl – I mean sheesh! Wasn't I just trying to get down with the homeboys? – It's like, burn all the ships, mates, there will be no falling back – Ho!

The pleasures of specialized mornings all running to crazy hot in this dopey life – The pretty celebs feed us with the pond scum of their weary lives while the ubiquities of dung keep getting bad raps from the Martha Stewart faction ...

Take my former bank manager as an example – One insolent afternoon I walk in and nail him about a heinous accounting misstep re: my funds – He vaguely listens, then summarizes his position with a dismissive "Modern life just sucks, doesn't it?" – I stare him down, rise up to my full vertical limit, make a wipe-the-ass motion with the checkbook, and fully assert that the account is now closed – My pappy always said an insolent dismissal should always be matched by one of equal value ...

Anchor

Not wanting to strangle in the success that blows in suddenly and decides to stay, I choose to sit with strange creatures in familiar places – This way, through the roof of noon, daily measures can be custom made - Of course where there should be the commerce of fire, we now have the dubious worship of advertised monsters – By this same vector of dodged success, I stumble on in an orphaned style, with more gurgling in the drain shadows, more swearing by witty abatement ...

Clumps of rare silence begin to efface the neighborhood cacophonies – The usage of oblique language also helps to dispel these burgeoning insanities – Holding steady by continuous change, this passing smile of yours remains the anchor ...

Scars, etc.

Ellipsis opens up the horizon of the unobvious, like: what is the sound of washing hands? – If you multiply the impossible by the absurd, you *will* receive plenty of incomprehensible looks, trust me – As you run through the daily gears, it can all be downtime unless otherwise indicated – Perhaps as Mr. Beckett gamely indicated, it's all just Boy Scout stuff ...

My radius of irritation, now approaching a full diameter, tells these resolute feet to avoid the cracks – These heavy steps belie the intensity of sounds as the voracious synthesis of hours continues – To the question "Where am I at?", a chronic befuddlement is willingly confessed – Scars are and will be my kudos, this life an education by flaws – It is all this clean living that is surely taking its toll on me, even as the pestering circumstances insist on getting in the way ...

Ramble

The morning unfurls, plans drop, no quarter for illusion, breathing increases, attentions unsheathe, lessons get logged, thoughts listen for the unspoken, intents charm the habitats, remembrances flush on the out tide, dreams converse through slivered essence, shadows of the azure world reach to a sky vocabulary, the incommunicado waits out the restless psychologies, evidence inclusive in doubts about demise, this genesis of terrain in the necessity of morning, my eyes close in spite of solutions, ideas rampant with too much fatigue factor, the more the thrashing the less the fear of starting over, glimpses through windows now a portal now a promise, of shining worlds to come ...

Sticky Futilities

Haute fictions crumble under the new global disorder – For once, the philosophically inclined have little to say – Eventually, even the erudite may return to a fundamental orality ...

More fragile than porcelain objects, our daily focus reflects the various minds creating or destroying according to aversion delusion what-have-you – Scripts composed recomposed transcribed in the painted characters of unsublimity – People filling up the voids in their lives with baubles trinkets the sticky futility of casino obsessions ...

Once there was a paradigm of grace – Now there's what, just more murderous howling under the terrasphere's vulnerable veil ...?

Heads Up

Now, it's not that the questions undo the work, but rather that time continues to bleed the questions – Take super-fluous events for example – Usually we're talking just a load of shit, especially if gratuitous whining's involved – Can't really see that there's anything original about sin either, it just being part of the existence package – Wax job, nose job, hand job ... all just skewed pieces of the same aberrant puzzle ...

It also seems that if you don't grab onto something in this perishing flame called life, it'll most likely reappear and grab you around the throat in ways you would prefer not – Personally, I like to occasionally inhale some juniper smoke so the terms get designated and stay uncorrupted – This way, the strange will remain in the estranged, and in this outpost of the galaxy at least, we will maintain ourselves as the most universal of fools ...

My Side

Justice? – What the hell is that? – Propriety is now sanctioned only by what doesn't reek – Needed most is probably a Declaration of the Accursed, something to sustain us as we slog along through the treachery and deceit – Taking sides with the oracular pagans currently just makes sense – Perhaps an anointed state yet lies ready to ambush these careers in failure management – Any insistence on using inflammatory adjectives should then speak for itself ...

Similar to the way combat can knock the arrogance out of you, I try hard not to get lost in the cruel provisionals – My catechism has been the hallucinatory pursuit of visions via the supremacies of hell – As in: When we talk, our eyes do not meet – Our claws have become retractable for the times when we may need to slap ourselves – In this ill-defined moment, I'm thinking any quarrel that results will certainly not be between order & imagination ...

Don't Mess with the Mess

On the sidewalk, a blind man plays Celtic ditties with his tin whistle, his empty hat beckoning listeners – His is the abyss of daily unknowns, the experience of being impaled by hunger – Makes you wonder what the symbol for oblivion looks like when reality slams you so hard ...

This will-to-power thing has been invalidated by today's impotent personalities – That and Zsa Zsa's asshole mentality – The philosophers too have been freed up to refute their own auto-eroticisms – I mean, the hell with Being (really have had enough of that word) – If evolution wasn't so god-awful messy, do you think we'd still be here metabolizing away in this "combat soup" ...?

Really, the derangement of the senses establishes nothing – In spite of Lucifer's revenge, how is it that humanity has even managed to stagger along this far? – This quarantined household in which we dwell goes by the name of Damaged Goods – And if carbon is the backbone of this sloggy adventure of the damned, where then is the diamond ...?

Out of Range

The specter of contrivance in blazing weathers, the crucible of midnight leaning hard on eternity's starboard – How can there be an appointed hour when one keeps stepping in and out of that ever flowing river? – Either by death or moving to the next town, life keeps jumping through the next set of hoops ...

The solicitations of rebel angels no longer tempt even as the weight of indecision stupefies me, more sure than a sharp strike – Who needs theologies when every breath inspires an act of faith? – Meaning can be allowed back into mundane actions so eventually the downtime seasons eat the dust and move on ...

Transparencies

Pushing the spark round about the battling wills, creative discharge announces the schizogenic efforts, the wrongly assumed always rising in rebellion – How to gauge the luring lurking duplicities in the eyes? – For is it not the eyes which signal looming estrangement and the transparent wounds soon to skew any threshold of co-existence ...?

Love being an always unfinished act, the willingness to trust has its own trajectory – In this theatre of lassitude, the abyss is now plumbed and ready for use – Although some might infer a full frontal ignorance, adjusted for further zeros, it is usually the Transparent that gets overlooked, the porosities of alignment funneled through these scanning orbs ...

Finding a Need

More potent than inaccuracy, her hands interpret my paper visions, lubricate uncouth enthusiasms, anoint any number of situations – At this juncture, love powder has an undeniable working appeal – It is her salacious winks which beckon to the mystery of what-the-hell ...

Stripped down, the action keeps demanding more Willard's Hot Lube, all propriety be damned – This one really values her shouting, I mean shrieking – The emotional weather just gets absorbed as it keeps rolling in ...

Yet, the nervous asymmetry of post-coital eyes does not betray any links with previous denunciations – All my imagined burdens thereby hang limp with remorse *and* gratitude – That is, thankfulness just for the breakeven status ...

Going for Water

The blasting blaze of bright summer wounds the smug citizenry, any misfortunes now rework into unsuspected blessings – All retreats have been blocked by the tears of the Great Mother – No choice but for the angels to stand down as the fool's quagmire sucks away – Is this lost ground, or ground lost? – Those user-friendly *Mutual Torments* (consumer commodity) seem to be a hot seller these days ...

I remain out here in the buggy woods, rooted minus the roots – This does help out as life gets more heinous – To live in the branches, this makes one resilient against future wounds, albeit happiness does include public tears and suchforth – But, when you're digging a hole bigger than the one you're presently in, what the hell does any of this matter? – Consequences, well yes, sometimes they're just flat out inexplicable – By fleeing the battle, sometimes victory can be a sure thing ...

An Odd Mind

A poem in a testimony of waiting, silence working well as a tension whim –
Perhaps it's time to ingest more focus from the deepest corner of the gypsy's
voice – It does concern me, however, that drivel goes first class while poetry
gets stuck going as freight ...

I kickstart the morning with a mixed grill of chopped smoke and former life –
Twenty five cents extra for onions – My instincts continue to be my only
wealth, although I have been known to barter for toothpaste on an as-needed
basis – These projected joys will always be non-territorial ...

The business of ramble is whatever I make it, hunger now my paycheck – The
open road beckons with the rhapsodies of space as I break up light on the
anvil of language – Apoetic immunity seals my emancipation, this odd mind
yet awaiting validation ...

Art as Praxis as Art

Through Magritte's windows I gaze now upon an archipelago of missed opportunities – If I spend a lifetime staring out these windows, will this possibly assuage the aggressive contradictions that are now killing my feet? – As some people enthuse about their sufferings, deep wounded and self-indulgently lusty are traits that bolster *this* tragedy of flesh – The fields of my suffering have always been fertile, hence non-subtle – When the emotional imbalance comes on, I reflect on the shame of movie stars, gilding their crumble, their struggles assuring the next plague that comes in for a visit ...

The surface of events . . . is that what is meant by image? – When you're trying to get the ground into focus every morning, what the hell does a question like that even matter? – Drowning in stats and the imponderable moralizing such as we are, if anyone asks, just tell them the road show has already left town ...

Mea Culpa Non Est

My heart oozes pomegranate blood this Good Friday as the dwindling few continue to genuflect through the Nine Stations – Blessings come from obedience was the scripted dogma washed through our brains in those days – Having ditched the saints, my protection is now sanctioned via this turquoise wafer I wear around my neck – Daily soliloquies emerged from/as disjunctive babblings, tempered by just so much allusion/illusion of course …

Underpinning the dribbling holy water was a fricative faith, prayers mumbled out to the immaculate something or other, begot not begotten, the putrefaction of sanctity lip-synched through the sacramental nonsense, solemn dogmatics fermented in so much priestly excrement …

If the Vatican could steal the sunlight, believe me, it would be done as sure as Thy Kingdom Come …

Best Shot

My voice has gone on holiday – Every inflamed smile I encounter seizes me with noiseless cruelty, a wading through more hypocrisy than a temple full of Pharisees – Seasons of drought now the judge and jury of these woeful ways, just getting vertical each morning is deemed a victory ...

I shadowbox with the dead poets like nobody's business, this glossolalia tending towards poetic midwifery – This form of ontology requires the collecting of images, the moaning of eternity embodied in all this metamorphosis, intrepid striving driving it on ...

Later, beside the water-scoured rocks, I enter into the safekeeping of shadows, the western horizon retreating as the bell sounds of evening fade – How can it be that dusk is the inflection point where reverie and harsh fact collide and disconnect ...?

Nature Freak

Behind the smiles on the street, paradox and misunder-standings lurk and dwell – From down south, the birds return for a casual stay, their oscillating notes hanging like plums in the thick spring air – At every step, the sex of exploding blossoms dilates inquisitive nostrils – A traipse through the rhododendron forest, the softened light almost violet, triggers a memory of those two lost days of love in Pasadena – Days that could never be so remote as they are right now – Desire's alluvium had spread forth like blood across a cutting board ...

But back to the birds – Even as they migrate through the fertile air, towards a horizon edged with blue tables, the evening sky blazes gossamer in the Technicolor west – Any glimpse of the extra dimensions should negate all the previous theoreticals, the prime mover still working through the history of the present moment – By these working decrees is a new alchemy sanctioned ...

Days of Kemo and Gold

Once, time became so final I vetoed any and all tomorrows – The needles went in, the hope went out – The vulcan cocktail tore me up worse than birdshot – I wept more than once during that steep decline – A flesh in chains challenged all that was most mortal in me ...

Strange how it was words in an unintelligible order that restored me to health – Once rid of the igneous insults, my blood was returned to its Precambrian origins – It was, looking back, only myself who had been the adversary ...

Even with these cougar claws strung around my leathery neck, the work still gets done by plenty of desultory sitting around – The boring larvae of indecision defaults to more questions of inexact living – Life, death, what the hell – The only lingering issue now is how many more incisions this flesh would be able to take ...

From Homer to Hollywood

What of opaque things to come, swollen by fiery grace worthy sacrifice and all of that – The work of fossil fires no longer valid, I write this for unknown gods and the breath of love – Any rush to complain should not deter – These hands remain hidden for no good reason, witnessed by all those who fail to listen, the earth keeps trembling beneath all this bumbling disorder, the daily feed all tangled up in derisive martyrdoms, from Homer to Hollywood, the lurid rains continue to fall on this that & everything else ...

This syllabic initiative now proof that doubts can work as a creative engine – Self-intimacy is always a labyrinth, these prose poems rooms without a door – Writing can be a form of incarceration, as in: the tyranny of the blank page vs. a stoic determination to work something up – In one obscure life, a journey an oracle a book bursting the shell ready to sprout – By the fiat of light, the troubles of this world are no longer any match for poetry's devouring flames ...

Still living in the Santa Cruz Mountains, Matt Hill has authored two books of prose poems, several chapbooks, and has also edited a compilation of random quotations. The *Marshall Creek Press* series of avant-garde chapbooks (1995-97) was edited and published by him. One day, he still intends on making it to New York City.

Made in the USA
San Bernardino, CA
29 July 2015